Chris...

Sharp Hills

Indigo Dreams Publishing

First Edition: Sharp Hills
First published in Great Britain in 2019 by:
Indigo Dreams Publishing
24, Forest Houses
Cookworthy Moor
Halwill
Beaworthy
Devon
EX21 5UU

www.indigodreams.co.uk

Chrissie Gittins has asserted her right under the Copyright, Designs and Patents Act 1988 to be identified as the author of this work.
© Chrissie Gittins 2019

ISBN 978-1-912876-17-4

British Library Cataloguing in Publication Data. A CIP record for this book can be obtained from the British Library.

This book is sold subject to the condition that it shall not, by way of trade or otherwise, be lent, re-sold, hired out, or otherwise circulated without the author's and publisher's prior consent in any form of binding or cover other than that in which it is published and without a similar condition including this condition being imposed on the subsequent purchaser.

Designed and typeset in Palatino Linotype by Indigo Dreams.
Cover photo © Chrissie Gittins 2019
Printed and bound in Great Britain by 4edge Ltd.

Papers used by Indigo Dreams are recyclable products made from wood grown in sustainable forests following the guidance of the Forest Stewardship Council.

For my dear family and friends

By the same author:

Poetry
A Path of Rice
Pilot
Armature
I'll Dress One Night as You
Professor Heger's Daughter

Poetry for Children
The Listening Station
Now You See Me, Now You …
I Don't Want an Avocado for an Uncle
The Humpback's Wail
Stars in Jars
Adder, Bluebell, Lobster

Short Stories
Family Connections
Between Here and Knitwear

Radio Plays
Poles Apart
Starved for Love
Life Assurance
Dinner in the Iguanodon

CONTENTS

Dancing in Silchar

Travelling in India 11
Prayer Flag, Nainital.. 13
Leaving Nainital 14
Becoming in Kolkata 15
Parvati and Plane Corner.. 16
Who Knew 18
Dancing in Silchar... 19
45 Squadron's Christmas Dinner.................................. 20
Tea Garden 22
Operations Record Book 24

The Needful Inner Life of Birds 26
The Man Who Moved from Shetland to Glasgow 28
Always Know Where You Are On The Map 29
Frontiers 30
Rain in Nice 32
English at Eight O'clock 33
House.. 34
Dreams for Returning Souls 35
Where is Freya?... 36
Corbel Angel, Southwold Museum............................... 37
So You Think You Killed Your Daughter..................... 39
The Apology Lab 40
How to Sell Your Soul on eBay 41
The Dilruba Player and The Boy................................... 42
Peta's Child 43
There's a Baby on my Compost Heap........................... 44
Glut 45

Hedging Around Pissarro 47
Loquats for the South Circular 48
Holi 49
Indian Miniatures 50
Cyclamen and Primula, 1923, Winifred Nicholson 52
Stanley Spencer's Pram 53
The Girl Who Drew Snow Leopards 55
Hester Dances the Polka to Elgar's Asylum Band 56
Pathétique 57
The Table Decker's Daughter 58
Professor Heger's Daughter 59
Hari Kyo, 8th February 61
Satin Stitch 62
Sundays 64
No Salmon is an Island 65
Hot Renal Waiting Room 66
The Unconscious Room 67
Last Flight, Temporary Captain Eric Ravilious 69
Don't Bring Death To My Door 70
Neighbour 71
Clifton 72
An Agent Sings Me a Donizetti Aria from Il Pigmalione 73
My Niece's Boyfriend Couldn't Attend Their Wedding 74
Your Unknown Sister 75
Day to Celebrate You Leaving Home 76
I Carry You With Me 77
Though June I Light a Fire 80
The Unseen Life of Trees 81
NOTES 82

Sharp Hills

Dancing in Silchar

Travelling in India

Certain attentions to detail are not necessary
when travelling in India.

There is only so much insect repellent,
sunscreen and Antisan you can spread across your body.

Six boxes of Imodium may be five boxes too many.

If the memory card in your camera has 1,400 shots left,
it is unlikely you will need another.

Only specific articles of Rohan clothing deter mosquitoes.

You do not need to buy a cheap watch in case yours gets nicked
because it will always be either on your wrist
or on your bedside table.

You may not want to trouble the hotel staff
who sleep on blankets covered in sheets
on the floor of reception, to wake you at 4.30am,
as New Delhi Railway Station will come to
the first floor of Smyle Inn at 3am,
when three generations of a family, and baby, vacate.

Prior to this you will hear five strong lines of pee
hitting the toilet water.

You will not need to buy snacks at 5.30am
as you walk along Main Bazaar with its
feverish fires and chai wallahs,
as your hotel will have packed jam sandwiches,
a banana and an eggless fruit muffin.

Also, in addition to the tea, newspapers and vegetarian food

supplied on the train, a party of fellow passengers
who embark at Rudrapur will unpack a picnic
and present you with a serviette, spoon, and a paper plate

of puri, kachori, aloo subzi and jalebi.

Prayer Flag, Nainital

My prayer flag is a bed sheet
billowing from the balcony above,
it frames the lake, lifts and curls,
hides ruffled trees lining the horizon.

I have my father's legs,
I have his willow hands,
I have my father's Celtic skin,
I have his hair of sand.

Diwan drives, his mobile phone
fastened to his hand.
He talks and texts, looks up, looks down
as lorries haggle round the hair pin bend.

I look up, not down the valley drop,
or sideways at the daisies on the bank.
Monkeys sit there two by two –
as they did for you in 1944.

My father rowed against the wind,
he tasted cold milk at the bar,
he saw arms of Himalayan peaks –
so near they surely couldn't be that far.

Back home a tea towel is my prayer flag,
a gamchha spreads across my table as a cloth,
a Kashmiri shawl – dry cleaning recommended –
lies unopened in the hall.

Leaving Nainital

At twenty-two my father changed
out of khaki, put on a white wide-collared shirt,
V-necked jumper, his highly polished shoes.

He turned his camera to the lake,
catching the white yachts with their
sails reflected in the waves.

Posing by the water with 'The Gang'
there was time to take in clean air,
ponder the lake's sage green depths.

The temple bells still ring, rowers
reach across the lake, drivers honk their horns
with every breath. Practice gunfire rides

around surrounding valleys.
I hope you rested well at this hill station,
that your pals brought you cheer

so far from home, from the hill
at Holcombe which you loved to climb.
A single black and white striped sail leans in,

the monkey is gone from the top of the tree;
the balcony rail, warmed by the sun, warms my hand.
The car horns start an in-depth conversation.

Becoming in Kolkata

I have become someone
who sits on benches

for a long time,
who smiles at a girl

with a cloth on her head,
who smiles at other smiles.

I play with babies on buses,
young boys glance back at me

over their shoulders,
I am called variously by strangers –

'Sister', 'Auntie', 'Ma'am'.

Parvati and Plane Corner

I'm alone in the Asutosh Museum of Indian Art,
   apart from huddles of guards
      who are keen for me to write compliments

     in the guest book on each floor.
        From a parade of Parvatis
          I choose one to study –

          black basalt, 11th century, Agradigun.
            Her torso is broken beneath her breasts,
              one foot snapped at the ankle,

          the other half way up her calf.
          A blown out beauty –
          braceleted feet, elegant long-nailed fingers,

     she's surrounded by goat-creatures,
     dogs on pillow haunches, figures in tall hats.
Through the hole in her body I can see

     a plywood fuselage, three quarters of an inch thick –
     Waring and Gillow, Parker Knoll –
splintered and smashed.

Six feet away, a rudder –
   stretched with bruised Irish linen.
      They lie on singed grass,

        on the floor of a glade in Cachar.
          Over the hill at the airfield
            my father rests on his charpoy,

Glen Miller plays on the gramophone –
>	*The Story of a Starry Night.*
>>	He's spent his day renewing fish glue

>	on the spar of a Mosquito.
>	Outside, he checks the coming stars,
>	lights up a cigarette.

>	He's yet to hear about the fuselage in the glade,
>	the bamboo leaves stroking the rudder,
>	his pals the pilot and the navigator,

who sat touching, side by side.

Who Knew

Who knew when
two pigeons
flew
down the nave
of St Paul's Cathedral
in Kolkata
while a Bengali Choir
sang Auld Lang Syne
that flying could become an art in which we can all partake?

That an egret with his wooden feet
can curve down
a shivering river,
that parents
married for fifty-one years
can grow feathers,
and swoop above
a congregation
of disbelievers.

Dancing in Silchar

In the Hotel Riya Palace goldfish swim around reception,
resting in the creases of the red leather sofa.

I show the manager my father in black and white –
here he is with a Vultee Vengence in Alipore.

In 1942 he liked to photograph the sharp hills of Chakrata,
his friends hold pineapples at Kumbhirgram –
a mere ten miles from here.

Does he know the Retreat Club here in Silchar
where his squadron came to dance?

Its new name is the Cachar Club,
but still my father is waiting,

his epaulets lying flat against his jacket,
two scalloped pockets at his chest.

He takes my hand, rests his other on my back.

My palm absorbs his warmth, his shoulder's strength.
As we spin across the polished floor
by turn I glimpse

the fronds of palms, and violet hills applauding
through the open door.

45 Squadron's Christmas Dinner, Kumbhirgram Air Base, 1943

Honeychurch-Jamchapel got on a plane
to replenish the food and booze, again;
the excuse he gave was the urgent need
for bomber parts, to maintain speed.

The deal with the crew was a glass or two,
small price to pay, so off they flew.
The soft blue mountains looked like the sea,
white foamy clouds lay in their lee.

At Calcutta the carpenter banged out the crates,
two contained pigs, with different fates.
Trussed and lashed they lay on their side,
legs protruding, tightly tied.

Pig 1 was OK and survived the flight,
Pig 2's leg was severed – the lashing too tight.
Could the Medical Officer make up a peg,
so the pig could scrabble on a brand new leg?

'No', said the Medic, 'he'll have to be killed.'
'Loose half our dinner?' They weren't too thrilled.
There followed discussion, a solution was found,
he would be jointed, then he'd be drowned

in a brine bath till Christmas, in the sick bay.
And what would the squadron be willing to pay?
For butchery and secrecy – a bottle of whisky.
The matter was settled, and concluded briskly.

With the prospect of boiled bacon and roast pork to eat,
you might think the dinner was now complete.
A sty was constructed for Pig Number 1.
But in a few days, Pig 1 was gone.

A crew was dispatched to search through the jungle,
'Dead or alive, shoot to kill, don't bungle!'
The pistol shots frightened Pig Number 1,
his surrender was instant, he didn't try to run.

The Christmas dinner was a huge success
with tables laid out in the Sergeants' Mess.
The sick bay staff supplied spotless sheets,
swopping table cloths for beer and eats.

The cutlery and glasses were highly polished,
the rules of entry – temporarily abolished.
Officers and corporals at this Assam aerodrome
toasted the Squadron, the King, and all those back home.

Tea Garden
for Jayanta, Urrunabund Tea Estate

In the valley was a perfect hummock,
each tea bush outlined by the dark space between,
flushed with golden light late afternoon.

To the right, a loop of smoke hung above the trees
almost reaching an ellipse.
You said the air was denser

now that winter was on its way,
so smoke took longer to disperse.
Winter means no picking.

The rhythms of two leaves, one shoot give way to
maintaining the estate – planted by our men,
before they left their bairns behind.

Will you keep on stopping in your tracks
to watch the jackal and the rooster?
There will still be problems to solve

requiring drives to the edge of the plantation,
to smoke a pipe, and watch the dragonflies
flit across the Borail Ridge.

As snow falls on England
you will strengthen the soil with lemongrass,
plant avenues of acacia, saw the lower branches to pegs

for pickers to hang their bags.
The lotus flowers on the lake open
their cerise petals at the top of long stems,

your line of petunias beside the bungalow will bloom
with magenta bougainvillea.
The leaves on the bushes will wait till spring.

'Two leaves, one shoot,' the blue throated barbet sings.

Operations Record Book

My dad is housed along a road of hibiscus, hot lips salvia,
giant spiked agave.

Swans and cygnets paddle before the vault which clasps
seven years of his precious life.

I must make up a code to store my bag behind a clear door.

Kit: Only sufficient necessary for journey duration five days.

I chose this day because I know it will rain from end to end.

The heat is terrific, we are not used to it, but the boys worked like tigers.

Still cold, I keep my coat wrapped round me
as I forget to tick 'terms and conditions' to become a reader.

Dress by day: Shorts, shirt, shoes or boots, steel helmet and respirator.

I queue again to pick up my ticket.
It will take forty minutes to order up material.

An enquiry revealed that one of the squadron aircraft has crashed.
No indication as to extent of damage and/or casualties
was forthcoming and the absence of information
naturally brought anxiety to personnel.

Two brothers from New Zealand look online for their
grandfather. An Australian couple want to know
why their uncle was in and out of the military hospital.

Six Vengeance aircraft bombed stores and Japanese H.Q. at Kalemyo.

I'm relieved to find that I can download the documents.
When my screen goes blank an advisor notices
and brings it back to life.

*Verbal information was received to the effect that aircraft
Mosquito No 811 had been involved in a crash,
and that the crew were safe.*

My father lies along the valley of the Irwell in the foothills
of the Pennines, he would not have thought
to flick between computer screens in leafy Kew.

The squadron stood down today except for personnel on urgent duty.

I walk beneath the trees to dodge the rain all the way back
to the quiet station.

The Needful Inner Life of Birds

I must walk quickly, with a frenzy of intent,
before the sand becomes devoid of crustaceans.

I must fly over glass waves spying shoals of fish,
only then can I dive like a rocket.

I must stand with my wings high in the air displaying
my white flashes, impressing.

I must shit on the French windows of the artist
as she looks out at sea.

I must lay my eggs in a nest of broken white shells
in the middle of a tombolo despite the boy on his quad bike.

I must glide with balletic grace around cliffs,
skirting the cavern, startling the tourists who rest at its rim.

Noss

It's not easy to photograph an island –
    the spongy sphagnum moss beneath your feet,
  mauve marsh violets beside a stream,
     a gannet shutting wings against fuselage
just before he hits the sea.

The wide ewe wades along an ancient path
    about to birth her twins,
      she's safe on the west side of the dry stone dyke.
   To the east great skuas pose,
  flagging their high striped wings above the buffeted moor.
     They're keen to feed on newborn lambs.

Lichens ring stones, three Op Art eider ducks
    settle on worn ledges shelving to the sea.
  Noss Sound laps and slaps the rocks
keeping Bressay at bay.

The Man Who Moved from Shetland to Glasgow
for Bruce, who opened a window in Glasgow
and wondered where the wind was

Where is the wind?
It's lifting sand into river veins
which hover above the beach.

Where is the wind?
It's throwing up gobs of froth –
they dance up basalt cliffs,
flee across sheep-shorn downs.

Where is the wind?
It's lashing the cars on lonely roads
where heath is cut with peat-black wounds.

Where is the wind?
It's flattening the cotton grass to red,
it's flipping leaves on strained branches,
it's whipping up white lace shawls on slate blue sea.

Always Know Where You Are On The Map

That way you won't miss the heron
as it soars behind branches,
glides across pummelled sky.

You'll witness the cows coming and going
in curiosity,

Himalayan Mountain Balsam standing sentinel
by the river waiting to fling
split pods into mud.

You'll notice a slight flush of red on the rowans
which will send you towards autumn
and away

from this criss-cross of dotted footpaths,
contours which wobble across uncertain ground,
fields which seem but are not

exactly the same.

Frontiers
for Teddy Buri, NLD

The Elsinore strawberries hung in their syrup
like air balloons in a red sky.
Seville orange slivers, marinated overnight

in Jameson Whiskey, lay cross-hatched
in gelatinous amber.
Carefully wrapped for the flight,

they nestled in my rucksack,
refugees from my overweight case.
But they were not allowed –

they might be explosive,
the percentage of liquid to solid too high.
I pleaded their case – presents for my host,

home-made. 'That's worse,' they said.
'Would you like them?' I asked the young woman
who tried to be kind?

'Not allowed.'
I'd like to think, at the end of the day,
when no one was looking,

she reached in the bin of disposed of possessions
and rescued my jars.
I hadn't lost my clothes, I hadn't lost

my childhood in photographs,
I hadn't lost my country.
And still it cut me to the quick.

As the plane lifted from my country
I thought of you fleeing to the border
with your life, only knowing

you were near to the camp
when you woke in the jungle
to the barking of dogs.

Rain in Nice
After listening to Bach's Goldberg Variations

My disdain for the rain on the Côte d'Azure
lasted only as long as the drizzle.
Grasping strength, it pelted the leaves
of lemon trees, skimmed the skins of olives,
laid boughs of bougainvillea low.

The fronds of palms trees dribbled,
umbrella palms dripped,
oleander blooms drooped,
the veil of rain thickened.

Then, still.

Until,
a flash of lightning stopped
all ice cream eaters in their tracks,
the deluge was back –
tripping down the tram lines,
trickling down necks,
trapped in open canopies,
gushing down the cycle tracks.

In its wake –
a blush of petals on the glossy pavement,
a sea restored to cerulean,
keen air, fresh enough to breathe.

English at Eight O'clock

Laying the leaf which fell on me
on layers of white tablecloth
I took my place in the middle of the room.

Two white-coated waiters served me
almond cake by turn,
my knife was moved by half an inch.

The tallest stood behind my back,
I could hear his catching breath
while men from Yorkshire spoke

seriously of walking;
the mountains flushed with pink,
anxious of the coming night.

All day – the watering of steps,
the positioning of shutters,
the placing of sachets by the bath;

until, at eight o'clock, English arrived.
Words purred up the stairs –
'reservation', 'credit card' 'the Valley of Oranges'.

'Bicycle hire' dropped into an empty vase,
'Vitamin C Express' aligned itself
along a polished ledge.

At midnight the receptionist slipped away.
'Naranjas', 'estación', 'de nada'
were murmured over the jasmine hedge.

House

It was something to do with your front garden
                          being almost a potager,

with the possibility of cavalo nero sprouting
            next to a salvia salvaged from a skip,

it was your white-covered white-seated sofas,

the reclaimed cupboards slotted beneath marble
                where you crafted a deeply felt pie,

which meant that in sleep I felt able
      to land on your doorstep

turn the brass handle,
    climb the painted stairs

and enter your delicious room.

It was also the reason I spent
      the rest of my dream in the doghouse.

Dreams for Returning Souls

To dream that a borrowed blue dinner service is carefully smashed,

that one season replaces another,

that a dead parent wants more of your time,

that your ladybird poppy seeds will never germinate,

that if you'd said the right thing he might still be here,

that, contrary to the mechanic's assurance, your new car door will not arrive from Europe,

that actors won't speak your words,

that you will never be fluent in Spanish,

that the weight of the osteopath on your spine will not be enough,

that one misunderstanding follows another,

that you didn't tidy your room,

that you were lost on the internet when the
blood orange marmalade burned,

that goodness leads to misjudgement of character.

Where is Freya?

I look for you on the red staircase,
under your mother's blackcurrant bush,

beside the pink campion in the tender garden shade.

I stroke the surface of the trampoline
for the imprint of your sole,

search your old room by the bathroom
where toys which tripped your games lie still.

Are you by the floral teacups, beside the plate of scones?

Or in the yeast which lifts your father's bread? Perhaps you're
in the candlelight which wraps the Christmas tree,

or in the brush which coaxed your peat brown hair?
You're in conversations which took place day by day,

in the clothes you wore for school, a new skirt for Saturday.

You're in the scenes you've left behind,
in the rain that comfort brings,

in sweeping valleys where the clouds drift by
and a knowing blackbird sings.

Corbel Angel, Southwold Museum

I am the pain of ages,
rivers and crags run up my back.

Ravaged by the beetle
I've been watching death since 1476.

Found in a thick green bag
on a tall cupboard at St Edmund's

my infestation was stabilized.
I take my wrongful place in this glass case.

My scarred mouth still murmurs,
my bitten nose still breathes.

The clatter of Dowsing's horses
rippled my skirts –

split now, like cracked earth.
The high angels escaped, unlike the rood screen's

twelve scratched faces.
I was not stained to match new timbers –

raised from a slab of local oak
I'm honey warm, longing for a glancing touch.

From my load bearing view
I could see snow flickering past windows,

knew that day would follow thick night,
that light would catch the flèche

and glint on unknapped flints.
Here I have a simple mission –

I lean forwards, in anticipation
of anything you care to tell me.

I can hide your secrets in my veins,
sift your frailties into sand.

So You Think You Killed Your Daughter

but here she is gathering sea lavender in the mist,
her damp curls blow into the corner of her mouth,
she stretches her arm towards the sea,
gulls circle overhead before making for the forest.
She walks the sandy path barefoot,
her bangles dangle round her wrist,
she sees her childhood friends
waiting in the dunes and breaks into a run.

You did not kill your daughter – she's here,
cutting through a piece of silk, winding it
around her waist, striding over the kitchen floor
catching shafts of light.

And if you think you killed your daughter
why is she here, packing a suitcase
with folded cotton skirts, slipping
new lipstick into a satin purse,
re-charging her camera and her phone?
She's looking through her window
at trees with leaves to give,
she's breathing in this certain air
and choosing when to live.

The Apology Lab

The cream walls peel and sweat with regret,
there's a graph on the wall to measure degree –
the date, the time, the century.
We pour coloured water into a grid of stoppered bottles,

watch each meniscus settle – black, brown or Prussian blue;
though a woman did try cerise one wet Wednesday.
We mumble as we pour, incantations of reproach –
the medication we could not afford,

the expectation we could not reach.
If the chasm is not too wide some write a note,
'I hope I would do it differently now',
then post it in the box beside the bin.

Each two hour slot sees a queue of new supplicants –
heads bowed, hands pushed deep in pockets.
There's tea to purge – with birch leaves, goldenrod and
marigold; shortbread biscuits well past their sell-by date.

As the second hour progresses eyes begin to lift to windows,
shoulders lower, movements quicken.
In the outer chamber Arvo Pärt is played, then Bach.
By then we smile,

sigh, try to fold away the past.
There's even laughter when a mobile rings out
Joni Mitchell. We say goodbye,
resolve never to meet each others' eyes again.

How to Sell Your Soul on eBay

Assemble with gauze, muslin, glitter
on a slender wooden plinth,
take a trembling photo,
treat as a rare collectable,
the new listing icon will burn at its side.

You will receive inquiries from
a homeless man in Walsall who warms himself
against the radiators in public libraries,
a man who torments his child,
a teenager who prises her veins.

These can all be taken seriously.
But beware the manager of an organic farm,
the dental nurse who offers new recipes,
the man who counts the plants on a given piece of land.
These may conceal a cloven hoof.

When your youth returns,
your love responds to your advances,
your children turn safely thirty,
then you may linger on the slate lake of content.
But a speedboat will sail too close

overturning your fragile dinghy,
you will float in and out of the freezing wake
while the heavens leak their beauty.
There may be help at hand on the shore,
or the beach may be completely empty.

The Dilruba Player and The Boy

A blind musician plays the dilruba,
sad sounds come from the strings.

A boy in a wheelchair appears in the audience,
his chest is congested – he wheezes and cries.

He cries and he wails –
the musician can hear him.

Moving his bow over the strings
he echoes the cries of the boy.

The boy cries once more, the musician replies,
the boy silently smiles.

Peta's Child

How high the swing?
How accurate the measure?
How deft the puzzle?
How soft the feather?

How comforting the crib?
How sincere the wish?
How sweet the lullaby?
How deep the hush?

How close the umbilical cord
To her heavy head?
How strong the amnion?
Enough blood fed?

How long to click your fingers?
How long is a bird in flight?
How long for a leaf to fall?
How long does snow stay white?

There's a Baby on my Compost Heap

her back is firm and warm,
she's curled up on the clippings
between flower heads and thorns.

Veins of root grow through her velvet skin,
woodlice make a trail along her spine,
a worm lies spiralled in her open hand,
slugs criss-cross her chutchy legs with slime.

In time she's going to lift her head
above the rotting leaves,
the wind will dry her tumbled face,
her breath will melt the rime.

Glut

  Too eager to show, I lay ten weeks
   tipped up in my mother's womb,
    poised to slither down a slide or glide
     around a helter-skelter on a scratchy mat.
      Now, when a gun fires, my feet
       stay on the blocks, I have trouble
        with digestion, my ideas glut
         like a drain choked with chicken fat.
          There are three houses in abeyance,

seventeen destinations to reach,
 a deal of ingredients for cake
  seeping from the cupboard.
   I like to slip the clutch at traffic lights,
    hug the wrapping on a present
     and leave it for a week
      till its content loses meaning.
       My favourite lesson was growing crystals
        on gritty string – they hung

in glass beakers the length of the sill,
 throwing gobs of blue across the walls.
  The words for love are compressed in my gut,
   'longing' lies across 'arms',
    'want' sprawls deep
     under a pile of diphthongs.
      Next month I'm going to
       wretch up and mouth
        sequences of the sweetest of lyrics –
         enough to woo anyone who waits.

W. H. Auden Got Married in Tesco (Ledbury)

Dearly beloved, we are gathered here in the sight of
Steak Fajitas and Hoisin Duck Wraps to join together
this Mann, and this man, in holy matrimony.
As we stand here between Meal Deals and Price Drops
wilt thou have this Ripe and Fresh woman to thy
wedded wife, even though you've never
set eyes on her before in your entire life?
And wilt thou have this man to thy wedded husband,
whom you wrote and proposed to,
in fear of your life, receiving
a one-word telegram in response –
'Delighted'?

For as much as Erika and Wystan have consented together
in holy wedlock, and have witnessed the same
before Coleslaw and Dips and Speciality Meats,
I pronounce that they be Man and Wife together,
and fully endorse Wystan's encouragement that
homosexual men marry European refugees
with the aim of political asylum.
So if there is anyone else hanging around in Savoury Biscuits
or Anchovy Fillets please do come forward.
And now go forth to Carbonated Drinks and Celebration Cakes,
be blessed and preserved and looked upon
with flavour.

Hedging Around Pissarro

New to the largest city in the world,
    where your wife refused to believe
        this chain of curious sounds
            could be a language,

you escaped cot and steam to set up
    your easel in the midst of winter.

Branches you thinned to cloud
    now are thick with brush;
        roofs, planed with snow,
    stand here still, staggered up Fox Hill,

though the drama of your sweeping road
    is lessened by a flattened curve.

Clouds are breaking into blue,
    as they did with you, but slanted smoke
        from chimneys does not rise.
            The staffage hovered discussing the thaw –

top hat, bonnets, long skirts –
    until the fragile light drained to dusk.

Today two men in tandem
    slip thin leaflets through each door,
    shoppers descend the slope with gamboge bags,
weighed down by the view.

Loquats for the South Circular

Between the satellite dishes and pink hydrangeas
of Stanyhurst low-rise grows a tree.
Leathery leaves reach out to lumbering buses
and ranks of council marigolds.

It fruits at the end of spindle fingers –
soft yellow plums, chuckling from
the highest branches.
It's July.

In China it would not show its hand till winter
when days have deep darkness on each side.
If you ask what gives me joy I'd say
this man from Guangdong

who opens his door to a stranger,
takes a ladder to his tree
and passes handfuls of his ochre orbs to me.
He gestures I should taste,

shakes his head when my teeth pierce the skin –
he shows me the way.
Back home, the skin peels willingly in strips,
it's obvious where the sweetness starts –

the pale flesh is soporific, juicy-dry;
the wet stone falls neatly in the bowl.
I take small bites,
then learn to eat each loquat whole.

Holi

A splodge of purple on your neck
and you can feel the temperature rising.

A rub of brown on your cheek
and your friend is your friend for ever.

A cloud of red above your head
and your feet start itching to dance.

A scatter of yellow on your shirt
and your enemy is now your friend.

A blotch of blue on your nose
and the winter is soon forgotten.

A bucket of black down your back
and you are ready to beat the drum.

A stream of orange in the air
and your heart begins to surge.

A smear of pink on your forehead
and your misdeeds fade away.

A dusting of green on your eyelashes –
spring is surely on its way.

Indian Miniatures

I Dhanashri Ragini Writes a Letter

The crane may turn back to his mate
in the nebulous sky,
I may not turn back to you.
Grey.

The fountain may shred water
into the indigo pool,
each droplet a speck on the surface.
White.

The fish may swim in concentric circles
never meeting at head or tail.
Yellow. Brown. Mauve.

The lotus flowers on my cushion
may point to the loquacious palms.
Gold. Pink. Gold.

My lady may look at me long
with her eager almond eye.
Black.

But my eyes are meant for you.
So take my painted words
and slip them in a birdcage.

There they will watch over you
while *you* watch pitted water,
claws of turquoise palms,

flirting darting cranes.

II Gauri Ragini Waits

I can sit in the limbs of this tree
and the branches are your arms,
the leaves are your fingers

glancing my skin – pale, they say,
as the champaka flower.

The importuning goats can ask, as I do,
when will you descend the white city?
When will we see you walk

by the devoted sheep, the delirious shepherd,
the sadhu deep in conversation?

When will my heart leap
as your footsteps draw near? The birds will
fly from the emerald trees, the monkeys

will chatter their news, while I make an avenue
with my wands of wishing-tree flowers,

strew champa petals in your way, reach out
my arms for you to lift me from
this too complacent bough.

Cyclamen and Primula, 1923, Winifred Nicholson

What is the tissue paper? Is it dun and bistre,

        a dash of baby ribbon blue?

And the cyclamen – do their petals

        flare with amethyst and wine?

The leaves are surely willow, cabbage, sage –

        stroked with fronds of sulphur.

The shadows on the sill flatten to khaki

        with a belt of air force blue beneath each bowl.

The peaks take turns to swirl in steel and pewter,

        the frosty sky dissolves to slate behind.

The ridge of window frame anchors with

        a pitch slash interrupted by two pots.

Though all painting, she'd have us know,

    are not pictures of objects at all,

but air and sky hanging onto colour and light

        for determined life.

Stanley Spencer's Pram

He collapsed my supple leather hood,
ripped the navy canvas stitched carefully
to my frame and smeared me
with cadmium, ochre, and a nasty shade of green.
Painting might have been
his way of saying 'Ta to God',
but it was my path to ennui!
I like to keep the wheels turning,
see a little of the world,
spot a few perambs around the neighbourhood,
check out *their* accoutrements.
'The May Tree, 1933' was bad enough –
all those cascading blooms needing to be caught
before they dropped,
but 'Gypsophila' (same year)
with days of dots and dabs for each and every flower?
It made me dour, deprived me of my spring.
When Patricia came on the scene I thought I'd rust.
Paint your second wife, naked as a baby
lying by a side of mutton?
I cowered in a corner of the studio
while he perfected tufts of pubic hair,
light falling on his collar bone,
her nipple stretched towards the joint.
Not a patch on Hilda, everyone said the same,
and how he did complain about those landscapes!
P. insisted – three a month,
and in exchange she'd hand a cup of tea,
offering her other hand to kiss. That's after this –
evacuated from her body, *and* his home.
The note lying in that case is his last,
written when he could no longer speak,
angels showing him the way to heaven.

What do I miss now I'm stuck in this museum?
The rushing of the river,
the spread of cedar trees,
cranesbill waving on the moor;
children calling by for autographs,
the way his glasses magnified one eye.
And in the dark – the daylight bulbs
shedding blue for painting through the night.

The Girl Who Drew Snow Leopards

Her words don't come easily,
there are gaps in her answers in class,
spaces filled by bared teeth and snarls.
At home her pencil glides across cream paper,
mark after mark make a dappled coat,
black stippled strokes hold a forehead,
the poise in a substantial tail.

She colours in pale brown eyes
as she leaps across the Kunlun Mountains,
she colours in olive green eyes
as she eschews all notion of prides,
she colours in ice blue eyes
as her fangs penetrate the neck of a stunned blue sheep
and they slither down lavender shale.

Hester Dances the Polka to Elgar's Asylum Band

Her fellow patients sit around on hollow chairs
gazing at the Malverns through the quivering window.

She brushes down her dusty skirt,
closes her darting eyes for one steadying breath.

Her right hand reaches to clasp another hand,
her left hand rests on the ridge of an absent shoulder.

Alone, she dances through a marriage,
her feet weave over the yielding floor,

viola pitches and swoons beneath cornet –
it's note held like a lark's hovering in the roof of the sky.

She stumbles. Her fall is broken
by a man who does not speak.

He takes her hand, rests it on his shoulder.
They dance, taking the piccolo by surprise.

The euphonium heaves all evening.

Pathétique

The piano stood upright in the front room
framed by the rubber plant
as it made a run for the ceiling.

Practice weighed in between homework,
table tennis, wandering the lanes to get a view
on the smoking town.

Lessons were a grind.
A small white bust of Beethoven
glowered from Mr Hamer's piano.

My father, proud to have a daughter at
the grammar school, sang in
the Rossendale Male Voice Choir –

'Glorious mud', 'Mad dogs and Englishmen',
'There is nothing like a dame'.
He played the tape as we drove.

I played his 78s in secret, thought that Humoreske,
played on a Liberal Jewish Synagogue Organ,
was pronounced Humorsquē.

One Friday, late in November, he came home
with sheet music from the city –
Beethoven's Sonata No 8, the Pathétique.

I sat down at the piano, opened
the thin folded paper.
The Key of E Flat Major – B flat, E flat, A flat?

Too hard for me.
Then, I only knew the key of C.
I placed it in the stool, beneath the studded leather lid.

Adagio, Daddy, Adagio.

The Table Decker's Daughter

Chewing on the word – *Marmotinto, Marmotinto,*
windows shut, doors snicked,

he sprinkled sand from a pleated card,
held close to make a rosary,

further for the leaves of lilies.
I ground glass, stained sugar, collected crimson

from the gravel pit for the mouths of snakes and eagles,
coal black for a tiger's stripes.

For a moment, before the guests sat down,
I could watch silica glimmering in candlelight.

Too soon, when all that was left were bones and stones,
it fell to me to whip the cloth away

and shake a veil of grey through an open window.
Is it any wonder he fell back into cake?

When the castle cat sat on his creation he threw
his box of colours to the ground.

I found him weeping in a pool of palest blue.
He's content now with jumballs, biskets, candied fruits,

though once I caught him, eyes closed,
throwing his arm in arabesques across the kitchen floor,

dropping stags and mountain sheep
beside the open door.

Professor Heger's Daughter

The first came in July when the canopy of leaves
cooled the garden in the afternoon,
she laid the pieces on the table
like islands floating on the green chenille.
Taking paper strips she strapped the words together,
a coral blush rose in her cheeks.
I shall see you again one day ... it must happen since I long for it.

Mother found the second in October,
leaves were crusted then with rust.
She pulled the river tears together with feather stitch,
white cotton whiter than the page,
the thin paper showing Charlotte's
shadow words behind.
– my sisters are keeping well but my poor brother is always ill.

In January, when threads of silver birch were
stained with plum my mother found nine pieces
nestled next to last year's invitations.
*If my master withdraws his friendship from me entirely
I shall be absolutely without hope –*

Another in November, leaves rotting in the rain.
I loose my appetite and my sleep – I pine away.
This was the last.
I know what it is to love a man and not be loved.
But to see my mother's eyes remember pain?

When my father lay on his deathbed,
his skin wax, his hands clammy and limp,
I flung the letters in his face.
'Did you love her? Did you ever love her?'
He screwed his strength enough to toss them
in the fire.

He found his peace in death.
I keep the letters locked beneath my bed
in a polished leather case.
It's only in the spring I take pleasure in the trees,
I stroke the buds and stems and will the curling leaves
to unfurl into sunlight, to bring a fragrant ease.

Hari Kyo, 8th February

Into the panna cotta I plunge paperclips –
       they've held me together in a paper storm,
             helped me to make sense of sequences.

I push in my empty Mitsubishi uni-ball –
       it's written itself out, telling of a long lost warrior
             smiling towards me in a storm.

I plant a line of post-its with out-dated notes –
       'noble, elegant, gracious',
             'turn right at the B2214 Avery Hill Road'.

I pitch a cracked coaster,
       where lemon and ginger tea, and coffee,
             have balanced fact from fiction day by day.

And last – a hair slide in two halves.
       It used to clear my brow
             to dwell on purple hills, and valleys caked in snow.

Satin Stitch

I run my fingers over the raised shapes
where your fingers pulled through
compliant skeins on rainy afternoons.
Pictures, tray cloths, cushion covers, serviettes –
you gave them as presents,
silky with satin stitch;

petals picked out in orange and ochre,
centres of burnt umber,
sinuous emerald stalks in slanted stem stitch.
Watching the acer swaying in the wind
planted for your poorly granddaughter,
you must have wondered where all life had gone –

the cul-de-sac quiet till the work day was done.
You'd add up numbers for the firm's accounts;
that evening Dad would add them up again.
You'd set about the story of your life
I asked you to write –
the apple wallpaper hung upside down,

the proposal in an air raid shelter,
the ring you flung back at your first fiancé.
You wrote instalments, posted them to me –
Best love for ever.
I wanted you to feel your life meant
more than just its blanks,

the times I helped you pack to leave your home –
a careful management of necessity.
You'd see it through with others on the ward –
the kind of friends you'd never see again.
Home first for a day, then two,
then pale days till the cycle spooled.

I use the cushion covers as tablecloths,
I like to keep your stitching near –
the cottage with the butter roof,
the yacht which smiles with nose and mouth.
The serviettes come out for notable occasions,
they feature in the art of deepest celebration.

Sundays

It didn't matter that we couldn't find the café
where we'd been before,
I thought it on the left, and you the right.

On we drove to Clevedon,
subterranean fish and chips in the café on the pier –
the only Grade 1 listed in the land.

Its arches, Bourgeois spider legs, prong the sea,
we walked along its turquoise length,
the day too overcast to see the hills of Wales.

It's on these days we consolidate the past,
we remember the red peony in the garden of our second home,
the tealeaves Mum piled on to make it grow,

the rhubarb by the tool shed in our third,
the goldfish frozen solid in the pond.
We're each other's precious reference book,

we hold complimentary notes to make a whole.
Your memories, written faint on scritta paper,
sound new to me, like stories never told.

Driving back we find the café, on the right,
closed down now, locked and boarded up.
We remember what we ate,

the fug and flavour of *that* Sunday afternoon.

No Salmon is an Island

No salmon is an island,
A bird in the hand is worth two in the brush,
A drowning man will clutch at a saw,
A fool and his money are soon to open a joint bank account,
A friend in need is a friend overdrawn,
An apple a day could equally be a pear, a banana, a
  mangosteen ...

A rolling stone gathers momentum,
As you make your bed, so must you learn how to do hospital
  corners,
Birds of a feather migrate South in winter,
Don't carry all your eggs in your pockets,
Don't count your chickens before they've crossed the road.

Fine feathers make a nice hat,
Fine words butter no pea sticks,
Great minds think independently,
He laughs best who has the best laugh.

Imitation is the sincerest form of phlegmatism,
In for a penny, in for a pound of penny toffees,
Let sleeping dogs lie in front of a log fire,
Look before you do a somersault.

None so deaf as those who will not wear their hearing aids,
No news is a technical fault,
Once bitten twice the teeth marks,
One swallow does not make a sore throat,
Out of the frying pan into the bacon sandwich,
Robbing Peter to pay the electricity bill,
Sauce for the goose is yum,
Where there's a will there's usually a dead person.

Hot Renal Waiting Room

My toes fluff into chef's white foam
standing in domes on the vinyl flooring,
my feet flood into gravy made red with Rioja;
my calves leak olive oil, unfiltered,
green and murky with sediment
tipping the ridge of the skirting board.

Are you a visitor to this country?

Thighs dribble to clementine juice
as orange as the marigolds at home
pulsing in my window box,
torso dissolves into dipping sauce –
Thai chilli and lime on one side,
jalapeno with peanut oil on the other.

We want to help. Don't abuse us.

Each arm vaporizes, dry ice billowing
through rows of flipping chairs,
my head – a bowl of Chantilly –
floats on a glossy pool reaching
the outpost of the noticeboard.

*Are you as involved in decisions about
your health as you would like to be?*

The Unconscious Room

Clothes are very important for an operation.
I wore mine for days afterwards,
like a uniform – a favourite brushed cotton shirt,

voluminous trousers, the right striped vest.
Not for me the anaesthetist's pale blue helmet,
the nurse's racing green V-necked short-sleeved top.

A royal blue curtain was my door.
In came visitors. The anaesthetist
who must take into account

a pre-existing condition in his choice of drugs.
The surgeon, who until he examines me,
is hopeful for keyhole surgery.

The consultant, who would like to remove
another, previously unconsidered organ.
The nurse, who says my text can wait

as she pulls on stockings, prepares me
as a mother would beneath my thin gown
held on with bows and ribbons.

And finally a man from Southern India,
who lets me finish my text, then
wheels me to the small unconscious room.

'She's been to more places in India than me!'
he tells the anaesthetist before he rescues
my collapsed vein.

'He's good. That's why he works for me.'
The tap on my hand is filled with
a crucial cocktail.

I wish I could remember the next few moments.
But what I do remember is what happened next.
The surgeon stripped to his underwear,

the nurse put on her hat and coat,
all attendant staff produced
canes and uncollapsed top hats.

They used the balloon pump on my tummy
and pulled out four fat links of sausages
through my open naval. Some knew

the dance routine, others not.
It was over in a jiff.
In the recovery room I whimpered.

'Was it keyhole?' The new nurse took a look.
'Yes, it was keyhole.' A host of red balloons
rose to the rippling ceiling,

a stray sank down onto my bed.

Last Flight, Temporary Captain Eric Ravilious

As you flew over craters filled with deep shadows
did you think of your cup of trees
greening the Downs? Or the bones of a hedge
stroked by rods of soft grey rain?

Tirzah, would you like a pair of gloves –
sealskin with fur on the back –
but what size shall I buy?
Draw your hand on the writing paper.

Were you meaning to cross hatch the skies
of Iceland, zigzagging the snow
on the mountains, repeating
the angles over the sea?

I am promised an expedition to see the geysers next week.
They seem to need soap to start them off.

Searching for a missing aircraft
your aircraft went missing.
Four days of searching found nothing.
Hope was given away.

You would like the country, especially the flowers and the seals.

When you were over the rutted ocean
black and swirling in the futile wind,
did you remember the curves of Cuckmere –
its deft meanders across a yielding plain?

I might collect some flowers for you.

Don't Bring Death To My Door

Don't bring death to my door
with all its intermissions.

Don't take away my spring flower meadow,
my honeysuckle weave,
don't taint the light mist on the horizon.

Leave me with soft dawns,
an endless supply of dreams
in which you don't feature
because it's you who comes to my door.

Neighbour
for Chris

He had already died many times –

in a snail thrown over the garden fence,
in the depths of his oxtail stew,

in the luxury items bought back from Le Sap,
in the folding fireguard around smouldering logs before bed.

He had stumbled on the baking beds of rudbeckias,
he had faltered while driving for early morning croissant,

he had fallen to his knees at the shrines of blue Mary.

His hands watered scarlet geraniums,
his voice soothed the voices of troubled children,

his fingers picked out notes at the funerals of strangers,
his ears heard a mobile ringing inside a coffin.

When the stairs were thrown back in his face
and the pavement caused him to limp,

his chair folded, took my neighbour back into himself,
while ladybirds halted on the laurel.

Clifton

I owe my life to the moon
dragging tides beneath the bridge –
low, high, low.

My feet were splayed on the parapet.
If I hadn't jumped I would've slipped.

The ships' masts rocked from Avonmouth,
Leigh Woods frothed with lime green leaves and May.

The first few seconds held all my knowable weight.

I tipped in somersault, the words of his letter
tippling towards the water.

'Dissolve' and 'partnership' broke the grey surface.
The photograph he returned of me

looped above my head,
my face saw everything I did not see.

Gusting wind billowed my caged skirt,
I glided diagonally towards Gloucestershire.

I would live if I wanted to or not.
In truth no man is worth that streak of terror.

Low tide, a bank of luscious mud.
Two passers by found me sitting,
guided me to brandy, a stretcher, a narrow hospital bed.

As I lay there watching ribs of light
progress around the room
my story bubbled through the town.

High tides healed my bruises, my null notions,
my toppled pride.

An Agent Sings Me a Donizetti Aria from Il Pigmalione as I Slice Carrots and Red Onion

We come from the same hills,
from an education lodged between pink sandstone
and Accrington red brick.

As he leans across the doorway
his cavatina slides along the kitchen surface.
He wants to re-cast me in the image of a novelist.

I would bring forth paragraphs,
a welter of well-thumbed pages,
he need never look back.

His vibrato fills the teapot,
the light is being chased from the windows.
My eyes sting, I slice my finger and the carrot.

He's grown impatient with triolets and sonnets –
if only I would sit at my desk day after day
so he can dream with impunity of turquoise seas,

cashmere suits, sleek wooden steamers.
Monthly he presents me with posies –
primrose, bluebell, peony, sweet pea.

He's been slipping sachets of Oregon Peppermint Tea
through my letterbox for weeks.
He's asked me in six different languages.

His smooth legato wraps around my etched water glasses.
The next morning there's an orange light
across the garden.

I pick up my pen – it writes itself.
'Chapter One'.

My Niece's Boyfriend Couldn't Attend Their Wedding Because He Had a Shift at the Holiday Inn

Sybil stood, taffeta drifting across her Doc Martens,
peering from the stone window.
The rain fell, the sun shone, the rain fell.
Siegfried was polishing the tea urn,
hoovering the carpet in Room 24.
Determined to wipe the smears off
all the windows on the ground floor
his fingers had started to wrinkle.

Sybil started to pace. She wore a track
from the front pew to the back.
Her curls began to droop.
Siegfried remembered he'd seen a dead wasp
on the second floor landing.
He dropped his wash leather and ran
towards the lift.
As he picked up the wasp

he had a vision of Sybil.
She was looking at cake tins –
different sizes. He popped the wasp
in his bucket and went back to his windows.
Sybil lifted her skirts
to climb the church tower.
She leaned over the thick sill and shouted
over the attentive town –

I do, I do, I do!

Your Unknown Sister
for Esther

She would've been your older sister,
an arm around, a hair stroke,
she would've made you laugh,

her strawberry blonde beside your brunette.
Going before she'd have kept an eye,
laid the way with her easy smile.

You may have squabbled –
another pair of feet to fight
for the bar beneath the dining table,

another face to vie for the bathroom mirror.
She may have borrowed your clothes,
you may have liked hers.

You live in the present –
your Fine Art degree imminent,
your prowess with chocolate coated gingers very clear.

Your sister is for ever in her fairy dress
or riding a patient pony, her cheeks
a mite too rosy as she struggles for her words.

Day to Celebrate You Leaving Home
for Esther

If I could padlock today to the Millennium Bridge
I'd lock the Thames saturated in grey,
the Shard blotted in mist,
St Paul's arching over a corner of the sky;

our discussion on the difference between art and craft
on the steps of the Turbine Hall
before we climbed to the Miró,
our laughter at the gouache
'Woman with Blonde Armpit Combing Her Hair
by the Light of the Stars'
in Room 7.

I'd lock our agreement that the quickest painting
in the National Portrait Gallery Award exhibition
was the best, your choice of
black hardback notebooks, green rubber,
and clutch of bargain canvases in the shop
with its annual sale.

And you, sat at my feet in the coach station,
your hair tangled and tamed,
your navel jewel glinting
behind your black lacy top.

I Carry You With Me

I carry you with me through security where, despite you saying
weeks ago they would have to be packed in a separate
polythene bag, I have to search deep in my rucksack
for moisturizer and 17mls of eye make-up remover.

Your empty seat makes a space between me and a man
who sleeps, and dribbles, through the entire flight.
(It's dribbling when awake I'd worry about.)

Past a glimpse from the Aerobus of the Placa D'Espanya
with its unlikely spaces and towers with beekeepers' hats.

Into the hotel room and the unfolding
of winter flowering jasmine and honeysuckle, pink verbena
and silver leaves which have all travelled well at 37,000 feet.

Up to the receptionist who tells me the word for 'subtitle'
is 'subtítulo' so I can ask at the cinema next door if
'La Vida de Pi' is dubbed in Spanish.
It is.

Through the avenues of oranges hanging on trees beside
the delicate arabesques of Christmas lights.

Into the Barri Gòtic and Santa Maria del Mar where the vaults
spur towards heaven and a man speaks into a microphone
of 'los niños' which can only mean Newtown
and buttressed despair.

On to the Picasso Museum, free after three on a Sunday, and
a tour of the rooms which ends in his riffs on 'Las Meninas'
in monotone and colour. A man sits on the bench
fingering his mobile phone.

Down the elevator where a man from Japan checks his neckline
twice in the mirrored door. His flies are undone.

To breakfast with tortilla and chorizo and a mirror opposite
the toaster where a Spaniard checks his silhouette,
turning from left to right like a toreador strutting his cape
as his soda bread browns.

On to the manageable Metro where a man stares at me long
and hard till I realize there is blood on my ticket.
I held it in my mouth and must have ripped off the skin
from my lower lip as I took it away.

To the dark green December leaves of the Parc de Laberint
and the hoops of the cypress maze where children
whoop and shout come lunch-time.

By the trickle of a one-trick fountain where I take off my shoes
and burn my face in the sun.

To the purchase of chicken and potato empanada and cheese
and cranberry tarta from the assistant who is eager to please
and desperate to take off her shoes.

To wait for the Number 24 bus to Parc Güell where
an elderly man goes through the bin
checking the dates on tickets.

On a night walk round the Old City where the contours
of the civic buildings in Place Saint Jaume are iced
with piped white lights.

Along the queue of people waiting to see scenes from
the Christmas Story staged in four giant windowed baubles.

To hear the blare of sirens heralding a demonstration against
the police who blinded a girl in one eye
on a previous demonstration.

To hear the children by the Cathedral sitting on the ground
under dark trees playing their recorders.

Past the elderly woman who sits, head bowed, cross-legged
on the Gaudi hexagonal tiles on the Passeig de Gràcia
proffering a paper cup. A framed photo
of her four children balances on her feet.

Into the hotel elevator which is filled by the previous person's
eau de cologne.

To see the woman with short grey hair and a plastic bag
at the 55 bus stop reading a small copy of Hamlet.
   '*Entran* Rosencrantz *y* Gildenstern'

To visit La Boqueria market where vegetarian, Thai
and Mexican food vie with thighs of Iberico ham.

I carry you with me to hear a disembodied saxophone playing
up the terraces of Montjuic.

Then I carry you home.
To a Lenten rose, a log fire leaping with flames,
and incessant unconscionable rain.

Though June I Light a Fire
i.m. Helen Dunmore

Though June I light a fire for you, and me as much
to keep the London rain at bay.

Not one whole day gone, you lie in Westbury-on-Trym,
more still this morning than you've ever been.

The paths which weave across steep Zennor hills
are being walked,

the waves at Porthmeor Beach are stepped upon,
The Downs are flecked with

children pulling kites,
runners stop to take in Avon Gorge.

Our last words were on The Downs,
and drinking tea at Caffe Arabica –

speaking of mattress protectors
and the luckiness of beauty.

Since then three times we missed each other,
slipping between a weekend already full enough,

an emergency hospital admission, and a date
too far into your illness – too late.

And yet you're here – as I peel a browned petal
from a rose, as a lime green caterpillar curls

against the curve of pink,
as the cold leaves are lifted by the wind.

The Unseen Life of Trees
for Esther and Jess

When the fraying skeins of silver birch
sway in the wind they think of
lulling water in the floating harbour,

the dried out plants on a deck,
the bespoke barge door cut to close
on a trapezium.

A sparse beech globe of yellow
holds an afternoon with two young friends,
who will walk through their vivid lives

beyond the end of mine.
A ball of mistletoe hangs
way up in spindle branches balancing

a trowel, a ginger cake,
and a framed copy of Jessop's 1802
'Design for Improving the Harbour of Bristol'.

Umber banks of oak climb the hillside
dragging children by the hand.
'There will be time,' they whisper,

canopy to canopy.
'There will be time, before
all our leaves stretch out across the frosted ground.'

NOTES

Parvati and Plane Corner (p16)
Plane Corner is an area in Cachar, Assam, where aeroplane wrecks from World War II have been found.

Tea Garden (p22)
During the Second World War many RAF personnel benefited from the hospitality of the British tea plantation owners and managers in the vicinity of Kumbhirgram, including my father; he stayed at a tea planter's bungalow for a week. The Urrunabund Tea Estate is very near to Kumbhirgram.

Corbel Angel, Southwold Museum (p37)
The angel was found during restoration work at St Edmund's Church in Southwold in 2014.

The Dilruba Player and The Boy (p42)
This poem was written after seeing Baluji Shrivastav playing the Dilruba at a 'Hear It Live!' session at the Horniman Museum 25th July 2017.

Indian Miniatures (p50)
After paintings exhibited at the Dulwich Picture Gallery in 2012 – 'Dhanashri Ragini of Shri Raga', Hyderbad, c.1760 and 'Gauri Ragini of Shri Raga', Rajasthan, c.1680-90. Artists unrecorded.

Cyclamen and Primula, 1923, Winifred Nicholson (p52)
In 1944, World Review commissioned Winifred Nicholson to write an article about colour. Wartime printing restrictions permitted the use of only three colours – red, yellow and blue. Winifred made a colour chart and invented words to substitute for the colours she could not print.

Hester Dances the Polka to Elgar's Asylum Band (p56)
Elgar wrote a series of polkas, quadrilles and lancers for the Friday night dances at Powick Asylum while he was Bandmaster there 1879-1884.

Hari Kyo, 8th February (p61)
Hari Kyo is a Japanese Festival for the old and broken needles of Kimono makers; the needles are laid to rest in a soft tofu cake. It is also a time to value the small, everyday objects of daily life.

Last Flight, Temporary Captain Eric Ravilious (p69)
A week after Tirzah Ravilious learned of her husband's death she received the first and only letter Eric wrote to her from Iceland, written in pencil. The quotes are from 'Eric Ravilious: Memoir of an artist', Helen Binyon, Lutterworth Press, 1983.

Clifton (p72)
Sarah Ann Henley jumped from Clifton Suspension Bridge in 1885 and survived.

Acknowledgments

My thanks to the editors of the following print and online publications in which some of these poems were first published: *The New Shetlander, Asia Literary Review, The Same, The SHOp, Obsessed with Pipework, The London Magazine, Poetry Salzburg Review, StAnza Festival 2015* website, *Southword Journal, The Lonely Crowd, International Literary Quarterly, Lakeview International Journal of Literature and Arts, The Punch Magazine, Poetry Society* website, *Horniman Museum* website, Kim Moore's *Sunday Poem* website, *South Bank Poetry, The Ofi Press*.

My thanks to the editors of the following anthologies in which several of these poems were first published: *Lyrical Beats* (Rhythm and Muse, 2012), *In Protest* (University of London, 2013), *Over Land, Over Sea: poems for those seeking refuge* (Five Leaves Publications, 2015), *A Poem for Every Day of the Year* (Macmillan, 2017), *Freedom: A National Poetry Day Anthology* (Macmillan, 2017), *Poetry for a Change: A National Poetry Day Anthology* (Otter-Barry Books, 2018), *She is Fierce* (Macmillan, 2018).

A number of these poems appeared in a letterpress pamphlet *Professor Heger's Daughter* (Paekakariki Press, 2013), illustrated with wood engravings by Helen Porter.

'Hedging Around Pissarro' was read at Kathleen Adler's illustrated talk *Pissarro in South London* during the Sydenham Arts Festival, St Bartholomew's Church, 9th July 2012.

'Dreams of Returning Souls' was part of the sound installation *I Leave This At Your Ear*, Southbank Centre Listening Wall for *Poetry International*, 2014.

'Cyclamen and Primula, 1923, Winifred Nicholson' was included by curator Jovan Nicholson in the exhibition catalogue *Winifred Nicholson: Liberation of Colour* (Philip Wilson Publishers, 2016).

'Corbel Angel, Southwold Museum' is displayed beside the subject of the poem in Southwold Museum.

My grateful thanks to the Society of Authors' for an Authors' Foundation Award which allowed me to travel in India for the month of November, 2016. Thank you to Helen Upcraft and Lynn Chapman at the Film Archive of the Imperial War Museum, to the National Archives at Kew, and to Keka and Jayanta Banerjee of the Urrunabund Tea Estate in Silchar, Assam, for their kind hospitality.

Many thanks also to friends who read and commented on the collection, and to Dawn Bauling and Ronnie Goodyer at Indigo Dreams for their unstinting support.

Indigo Dreams Publishing Ltd
24, Forest Houses
Cookworthy Moor
Halwill
Beaworthy
Devon
EX21 5UU
www.indigodreams.co.uk